WELCOME

On behalf of the Dynamic Catholic team and the local volunteers who have worked together to make today possible, we want to welcome you. We hope today will be a powerful experience for you.

Here are some suggestions for making the most of the event:

- **Congratulations!** We all need to step back from time to time and take another look at who we are, where we are, and where we are going! But too often, we don't – either because we are afraid of what we will discover or because we are unable to get off the treadmill of life. Just being here is a great first step.

- **The Big Decision.** There is one big decision you need to make today. Is today going to be a life-changing experience or just another event? You decide.

- **Be Present.** This is one of life's unchanging lessons. Be where you are. It sounds so simple, but it is very difficult. There are many other places you could be today, and many other things you could be doing. No doubt you have long to-do lists – both personal and professional. Set them aside for now. They will all be there tomorrow, and you will be better prepared for them if you immerse yourself in today's event.

- **Move Beyond.** Henry Ford wrote, "If you always do what you've always done, you'll always get what you've always gotten." Open your heart, mind, and soul to new ideas today, and to new direction.

- **Made for Mission.** Today is not just about you. It is about preparing you for whatever mission God has envisioned for you from the beginning of the world. We hope when you leave today you will be re-energized personally, but we also pray you will take this new energy and unleash it in your parish.

- **Have Fun!** We learn best and grow most when we are having fun. So breathe deep, smile, celebrate and enjoy the event.

- **Press On.** As you begin to live what you learn here today there will be many people who try to discourage you. Sometimes the people you most expect to encourage you, will actually discourage you. Never get discouraged. Press on. Whatever God calls you to today, etch it into your heart and mind, and move toward it every day for the rest of your life. Allow no obstacle to get in your way.

THE
DYNAMIC CATHOLIC
PRAYER

Loving Father,

I invite You into my life today
and make myself available to You.

Help me to become the-best-version-of-myself
by seeking Your will and becoming
a living example of Your love in the world.

Open my heart to the areas of my life
that need to change in order for me to
carry out the mission and experience the joy
You have imagined for my life.

Inspire me to live the Catholic faith
in ways that are dynamic and engaging.

Show me how to best get involved
in the life of my parish.

Make our community hungry for
best practices and continuous learning.

Give me courage when I am afraid, hope when
I am discouraged, and clarity in times of decision.

Teach me to enjoy uncertainty and
do my part to enable Your Church to become all
You imagined it would be for the people of our times.

Amen.

NOTES

NOTES

"WHO YOU BECOME IS INFINITELY MORE IMPORTANT
THAN WHAT YOU DO, OR WHAT YOU HAVE."

[MATTHEW KELLY]

"THERE ARE TWO WAYS TO LIVE LIFE. ONE IS AS THOUGH
NOTHING IS A MIRACLE. THE OTHER IS AS THOUGH EVERYTHING
IS A MIRACLE."

[ALBERT EINSTEIN]

"PLACE YOUR TALENTS AND ENTHUSIASM AT THE SERVICE OF LIFE."

[POPE JOHN PAUL II]

NOTES

_____

_____

_____

_____

_____

_____

_____

_____

_____

_____

_____

_____

_____

_____

_____

_____

_____

_____

_____

_____

_____

_____

_____

"OUR LIVES CHANGE WHEN OUR HABITS CHANGE."

[MATTHEW KELLY]

NOTES

_____
_____
_____
_____
_____
_____
_____
_____
_____
_____
_____
_____
_____
_____
_____
_____
_____
_____
_____
_____
_____

"COME TO THE EDGE," HE SAID.
THEY SAID, "WE ARE AFRAID."
"COME TO THE EDGE," HE SAID AGAIN.
THEY CAME. "HE PUSHED THEM... AND THEY FLEW."

[GUILLAUME APOLLINAIRE]

"THE GREATER DANGER FOR MOST OF US IS NOT THAT OUR AIM IS TOO HIGH AND WE MISS IT, BUT THAT IT IS TOO LOW AND WE REACH IT."

[MICHELANGELO]

_____

_____

_____

_____

_____

_____

_____

_____

_____

_____

_____

_____

_____

_____

_____

_____

_____

_____

_____

"I KNOW THIS NOW. EVERY MAN GIVES HIS LIFE FOR WHAT HE BELIEVES. EVERY WOMAN GIVES HER LIFE FOR WHAT SHE BELIEVES. SOMETIMES PEOPLE BELIEVE IN LITTLE OR NOTHING, AND YET THEY GIVE THEIR LIVES TO THAT LITTLE OR NOTHING. ONE LIFE IS ALL WE HAVE AND WE LIVE IT AS WE BELIEVE IN LIVING IT AND THEN IT'S GONE. BUT TO SURRENDER WHAT YOU ARE AND TO LIVE WITHOUT BELIEF IS MORE TERRIBLE THAN DYING—EVEN MORE TERRIBLE THAN DYING YOUNG."

[JOAN OF ARC]

"FIRST DO WHAT IS NECESSARY, THEN DO WHAT IS POSSIBLE, AND BEFORE LONG YOU WILL FIND YOURSELF DOING THE IMPOSSIBLE."

[FRANCIS OF ASSISI]

"ONCE FOUND, FORGIVENESS FREES. IT LIBERATES YOU FROM FEVERISHLY KEEPING SCORE AND REMEMBERING WRONGS. IT PROPELS YOU INTO A NEW, HIGHER WAY OF LIVING. A LIFE OF GRACE. A LIFE OF SECOND CHANCES."

[ALLEN HUNT]

NOTES

"THE SHORTEST AND SUREST WAY TO LIVE WITH HONOR IN THE WORLD IS TO BE IN REALITY WHAT WE WOULD APPEAR TO BE; ALL HUMAN VIRTUES INCREASE AND STRENGTHEN THEMSELVES BY THE PRACTICE AND EXPERIENCE OF THEM."

[SOCRATES]

"BE PATIENT TOWARD ALL THAT IS UNRESOLVED IN YOUR
HEART. AND TRY TO LOVE THE QUESTIONS THEMSELVES. DO
NOT SEEK THE ANSWERS THAT CANNOT BE GIVEN TO YOU
BECAUSE YOU WOULD NOT BE ABLE TO LIVE THEM. AND THE
POINT IS TO LIVE EVERYTHING. LIVE THE QUESTIONS NOW.
PERHAPS YOU WILL THEN GRADUALLY, WITHOUT NOTICING IT,
LIVE ALONG SOME DISTANT DAY INTO THE ANSWER."

[RAINER MARIA RILKE]

NOTES

"IF WE WILL WALK HUMBLY WITH OUR GOD, HE WILL LEAD US BY THE HAND TO EXACTLY WHO AND WHAT WE NEED, TO THOSE PEOPLE, THINGS, AND EXPERIENCES HE HAS DESIGNED AND INTENDED FOR US, AND THIS ALONE WILL BE THE CAUSE OF OUR DEEP FULFILLMENT AND HAPPINESS."

[MATTHEW KELLY]

"WE ARE NOT HUMAN BEINGS HAVING A SPIRITUAL EXPERIENCE. WE ARE SPIRITUAL BEINGS HAVING A HUMAN EXPERIENCE."

[PIERRE TEILHARD DE CHARDIN]

"IF BEING TOGETHER BOTHERS YOU, YOUR MARRIAGE IS
ENTERING THE DANGER ZONE."

[ALLEN HUNT]

_____

_____

_____

_____

_____

_____

_____

_____

_____

_____

_____

_____

_____

_____

_____

_____

_____

_____

_____

_____

_____

_____

_____

"EVERYTHING IS POSSIBLE FOR THE ONE WHO BELIEVES."

[JESUS OF NAZARETH]

_____

_____

_____

_____

_____

_____

_____

_____

_____

_____

_____

_____

_____

_____

_____

_____

_____

_____

_____

"LIFE IS ABOUT LOVE. IT'S ABOUT WHOM YOU LOVE AND WHOM YOU HURT. LIFE'S ABOUT HOW YOU LOVE YOURSELF AND HOW YOU HURT YOURSELF. LIFE'S ABOUT HOW YOU LOVE AND HURT THE PEOPLE CLOSE TO YOU. LIFE IS ABOUT HOW YOU LOVE AND HURT THE PEOPLE WHO JUST CROSS YOUR PATH FOR A MOMENT. LIFE IS ABOUT LOVE."

[MATTHEW KELLY]

_____
_____
_____
_____
_____
_____
_____
_____
_____
_____
_____
_____
_____
_____
_____
_____
_____
_____
_____
_____
_____

"SOME PEOPLE ARE GOING TO LIKE ME AND SOME PEOPLE AREN'T, SO I MIGHT AS WELL BE ME. THEN, AT LEAST, I WILL KNOW THAT THE PEOPLE WHO LIKE ME, LIKE ME."

[HUGH PRATHER]

"LORD, MAKE ME AN INSTRUMENT OF YOUR PEACE."

[FRANCIS OF ASSISI]

"ONE CAN CHOOSE TO GO BACK TOWARD SAFETY OR
FORWARD TOWARD GROWTH. GROWTH MUST BE CHOSEN
AGAIN AND AGAIN; FEAR MUST BE OVERCOME AGAIN
AND AGAIN."

[ABRAHAM MASLOW]

NOTES

"THE DICTIONARY IS THE ONLY PLACE THAT SUCCESS COMES BEFORE WORK. HARD WORK IS THE PRICE WE MUST PAY FOR SUCCESS. I THINK YOU CAN ACCOMPLISH ALMOST ANYTHING IF YOU'RE WILLING TO PAY THE PRICE."

[VINCE LOMBARDI]

_____

_____

_____

_____

_____

_____

_____

_____

_____

_____

_____

_____

_____

_____

_____

_____

_____

_____

"REMEMBER YOU HAVE ONLY ONE SOUL; THAT YOU HAVE ONLY ONE DEATH TO DIE; THAT YOU HAVE ONLY ONE LIFE, WHICH IS SHORT AND HAS TO BE LIVED BY YOU ALONE; AND THERE IS ONLY ONE GLORY, WHICH IS ETERNAL. IF YOU DO THIS, THERE WILL BE A GREAT MANY THINGS ABOUT WHICH YOU CARE NOTHING."

[TERESA OF AVILA]

NOTES

"WE WHO LIVED IN CONCENTRATION CAMPS CAN REMEMBER
THE MEN WHO WALKED THROUGH THE HUTS COMFORTING
OTHERS. GIVING AWAY THEIR LAST PIECE OF BREAD. THEY MAY
HAVE BEEN FEW IN NUMBER, BUT THEY OFFER SUFFICIENT
PROOF THAT EVERYTHING CAN BE TAKEN FROM A MAN BUT ONE
THING: THE LAST OF THE HUMAN FREEDOMS—TO CHOOSE ONE'S
ATTITUDE IN ANY GIVEN SET OF CIRCUMSTANCES—TO CHOOSE
ONE'S OWN WAY."

[VICTOR FRANKL]

NOTES

_____

"MEN STUMBLE OVER THE TRUTH FROM TIME TO TIME, BUT
MOST PICK THEMSELVES UP AND HURRY OFF AS IF NOTHING
HAPPENED."

[WINSTON CHURCHILL]

"A MAN WOULD DO NOTHING IF HE WAITED UNTIL HE COULD DO IT SO WELL THAT NO ONE WOULD FIND FAULT WITH WHAT HE HAS DONE."

[JOHN HENRY NEWMAN]

"THE TRUE WORTH OF A MAN IS TO BE MEASURED BY THE
THINGS HE PURSUES."

[MARCUS AURELIUS]

_____
_____
_____
_____
_____
_____
_____
_____
_____
_____
_____
_____
_____
_____
_____
_____
_____
_____
_____

"THE CHALLENGE LIFE PRESENTS TO EACH OF US IS TO BECOME TRULY OURSELVES--NOT THE SELF WE HAVE IMAGINED OR FANTASIZED ABOUT, NOT THE SELF THAT OUR FRIENDS WANT US TO BE, NOT THE SELF OUR EGO WOULD HAVE US BE, BUT THE SELF GOD HAS ORDAINED US TO BE FROM BEFORE WE WERE IN OUR MOTHER'S WOMB."

[MATTHEW KELLY]

"WHY IS IT SO HARD FOR SO MANY TO REALIZE THAT WINNERS ARE USUALLY THE ONES WHO WORK HARDER, WORK LONGER AND, AS A RESULT, PERFORM BETTER?"

[JOHN WOODEN]

"I SAID TO THE ALMOND TREE, 'SISTER, SPEAK TO ME OF GOD,'
AND THE ALMOND TREE BLOSSOMED."

[GRECO]

"I WENT TO THE WOODS BECAUSE I WANTED TO LIVE DELIBERATELY... I WANTED TO LIVE DEEP AND SUCK OUT ALL OF THE MARROW OF LIFE! TO PUT TO ROUT ALL THAT WAS NOT LIFE. AND NOT, WHEN I CAME TO DIE, DISCOVER THAT I HAD NOT LIVED..."

[HENRY DAVID THOREAU]

NOTES

"WHAT LIES BEHIND US AND WHAT LIES BEFORE US ARE SMALL MATTERS COMPARED TO WHAT LIES WITHIN US."

[RALPH WALDO EMERSON]

NOTES

_____
_____
_____
_____
_____
_____
_____
_____
_____
_____
_____
_____
_____
_____
_____
_____
_____
_____
_____
_____
_____

"CATHEDRALS AND CHURCHES ARCHITECTURALLY PREPARE OUR SOULS FOR THE BEAUTY OF THE EUCHARIST."

[ALLEN HUNT]

_____

_____

_____

_____

_____

_____

_____

_____

_____

_____

_____

_____

_____

_____

_____

_____

_____

_____

_____

_____

"DO NOT LET YOUR LIFE BE LIKE A SHOOTING STAR WHICH LIGHTS UP THE SKY FOR ONLY A BRIEF MOMENT. LET YOUR LIFE BE LIKE THE SUN THAT ALWAYS BURNS BRIGHTLY IN THE HEAVENS BRINGING LIGHT AND WARMTH TO ALL THOSE ON EARTH. LET YOUR LIGHT SHINE!"

[MATTHEW KELLY]

"THE UNEXAMINED LIFE IS NOT WORTH LIVING."

[SOCRATES]

_____

_____

_____

_____

_____

_____

_____

_____

_____

_____

_____

_____

_____

_____

_____

_____

_____

_____

_____

_____

_____

"WE BECOME THE BOOKS WE READ."

[MATTHEW KELLY]

"LOVE AND EVER MORE LOVE IS THE ONLY SOLUTION TO EVERY PROBLEM THAT COMES UP. IF WE LOVE EACH OTHER ENOUGH, WE WILL BEAR WITH EACH OTHERS FAULTS AND BURDENS. IF WE LOVE ENOUGH, WE ARE GOING TO LIGHT THAT FIRE IN THE HEARTS OF OTHERS. AND IT IS LOVE THAT WILL BURN OUT THE SINS AND HATREDS THAT SADDEN US. IT IS LOVE THAT WILL MAKE US WANT TO DO GREAT THINGS FOR EACH OTHER. NO SACRIFICE AND NO SUFFERING WILL THEN SEEM TOO MUCH. YES, I SEE ONLY TOO CLEARLY HOW BAD PEOPLE ARE. I WISH I DID NOT SEE IT SO. IT IS MY OWN SINS THAT GIVE ME SUCH CLARITY."

[DOROTHY DAY]

NOTES

"I EXPECT TO PASS THROUGH THIS WORLD BUT ONCE. ANY
GOOD THEREFORE THAT I CAN DO OR ANY KINDNESS THAT
I CAN SHOW TO ANY FELLOW CREATURE, LET ME DO IT NOW.
LET ME NOT DEFER OR NEGLECT IT, FOR I SHALL NOT PASS
THIS WAY AGAIN."

[WILLIAM PENN]

NOTES

"WHATEVER IS TRUE, WHATEVER IS HONORABLE, WHATEVER IS
JUST, WHATEVER IS PURE, WHATEVER IS PLEASING, WHATEVER
IS COMMENDABLE, IF THERE IS ANY EXCELLENCE AND IF THERE
IS ANYTHING WORTHY OF PRAISE, THINK ABOUT THESE THINGS."

[PAUL OF DAMASCUS]

NOTES

_____
_____
_____
_____
_____
_____
_____
_____
_____
_____
_____
_____
_____
_____
_____
_____
_____
_____
_____

"MY SON, CONDUCT YOUR AFFAIRS WITH HUMILITY, AND
YOU WILL BE LOVED MORE THAN A GIVER OF GIFTS. HUMBLE
YOURSELF THE MORE THE GREATER YOU ARE, AND YOU WILL
FIND FAVOR WITH GOD."

[SIRACH]

NOTES

_____

_____

_____

_____

_____

_____

_____

_____

_____

_____

_____

_____

_____

_____

_____

_____

_____

_____

_____

_____

"WE CAN NEVER GET ENOUGH OF WHAT WE DON'T REALLY NEED."

[MATTHEW KELLY]

_____

"DO NOT BE AFRAID."

[JESUS OF NAZARETH]

_____
_____
_____
_____
_____
_____
_____
_____
_____
_____
_____
_____
_____
_____
_____
_____
_____
_____
_____
_____
_____
_____
_____
_____

"YESTERDAY IS GONE. TOMORROW HAS NOT YET COME.
WE HAVE ONLY TODAY. LET US BEGIN."

[MOTHER TERESA]

_____
_____
_____
_____
_____
_____
_____
_____
_____
_____
_____
_____
_____
_____
_____
_____
_____
_____
_____
_____
_____
_____

"GREAT SPIRITS HAVE ALWAYS ENCOUNTERED VIOLENT
OPPOSITION FROM MEDIOCRE MINDS. THE LATTER CANNOT
UNDERSTAND IT WHEN A MAN DOES NOT THOUGHTLESSLY
SUBMIT TO HEREDITARY PREJUDICES, BUT HONESTLY AND
COURAGEOUSLY USES HIS INTELLIGENCE."

[ALBERT EINSTEIN]

"EVERY BLADE OF GRASS HAS ITS ANGEL THAT BENDS OVER IT AND WHISPERS, 'GROW, GROW.'"

[THE TALMUD]

"THE MEASURE OF YOUR LIFE WILL BE THE MEASURE OF
YOUR COURAGE."

[MATTHEW KELLY]

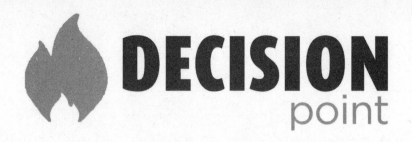

THE DYNAMIC CATHOLIC
CONFIRMATION EXPERIENCE

*"I am convinced this is the best invitation
to young Catholics to accept and live their faith
that I have encountered."*

— CARDINAL DONALD WUERL, Archbishop of Washington

REQUEST YOUR FREE* PROGRAM PACK
at DynamicCatholic.com/Confirmation

*The complimentary program pack includes:
the complete DVD series containing 72 short films,
the student workbook, and the leader guide.*

*Just pay shipping.

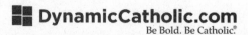
DynamicCatholic.com
Be Bold. Be Catholic.

_____
_____
_____
_____
_____
_____
_____
_____
_____
_____
_____
_____
_____
_____
_____
_____
_____
_____
_____
_____
_____
_____

"LET NOTHING TROUBLE YOU. LET NOTHING FRIGHTEN YOU. ALL THINGS PASS AWAY. GOD NEVER CHANGES. PATIENCE OBTAINS ALL THINGS. NOTHING IS WANTING TO HE WHO POSSESSES GOD. GOD ALONE SUFFICES."

[TERESA OF AVILA]

KEEP GROWING!

At Dynamic Catholic we are committed to helping you continue to grow. This event is just the beginning. Visit DynamicCatholic.com and you will find a lifetime of resources to accompany you in your journey. We are also constantly adding new resources to provide you with fresh ways to live with passion and purpose – so be sure to check back in with us regularly.

Here are **5 WAYS TO KEEP GROWING:**

1. USE THE PRAYER PROCESS.

Daily prayer is at the center of the Christian life. All our research at The Dynamic Catholic Institute reveals that developing a daily routine and discipline of prayer is the first step.

The Prayer Process is a simple way to develop a daily routine of prayer. Read about it at DynamicCatholic.com or in The Four Signs of a Dynamic Catholic (Pages 41-69). Then, place a Prayer Process card in your purse or wallet so you can take The Prayer Process wherever you go!

2. READ GREAT SPIRITUAL BOOKS.

Books change our lives. What we read today walks and talks with us tomorrow. If the ideas you heard today challenged you and comforted you, we encourage you to find ways to develop a constant flow of great ideas into your heart, mind, and soul.

The easiest way is through books. At Dynamic Catholic we are committed to putting the best Catholic books of our times in your hands.

Continuous learning and spiritual vitality go hand in hand. At Dynamic Catholic, we are passionate about helping Catholics become continuous learners, which is why you can request a [FREE] copy of dozens of books, CDs, and DVDs. Simply pay shipping and handling.

3. GET A MASS JOURNAL.

Every relationship improves when we really start to listen. Are you ready to really start listening to the voice of God in your life?

When you walk into Mass next Sunday, ask God this question in the quiet of your heart, "God, show me one way in this Mass that I can become a-better-version-of-myself this week." Then listen.

Better yet. Get yourself a small journal and write down what he says to you each week. Date each entry. You will be amazed how this one new habit can transform your spiritual life.

Our lives change when our habits change. Visit DynamicCatholic.com and request a [FREE] Mass Journal today.

4. BE THE DIFFERENCE.

There are so many people who need to hear the message you heard today. You live with some of them, work with others, some sit by you at church on Sunday, and others attend school with your children. There are millions of people who live lives of quiet desperation. They want to live with passion and purpose, but they simply don't know how.

You can make an enormous difference in these people's lives... and it may be much easier than you ever imagined.

At Dynamic Catholic we have discovered that simply giving someone a book or a CD can change the whole direction of their lives. We make it easy and affordable, offering six copies of any product in the program for just $18 (including shipping).

How many lives are you going to help change?

5. JOIN THE MISSION.

The Catholic Church is in need of renewal. At Dynamic Catholic we believe that millions of ordinary Catholics want to be involved in a movement that provides a game-changing strategy for the Church today.

We hope you will join us in the mission. Join us in our efforts to re-energize the Catholic Church by becoming a Dynamic Catholic Ambassador. Learn more at DynamicCatholic.com

Among the many benefits of being an Ambassador are the monthly spiritual coaching calls with Matthew Kelly. Like all we do, they are designed to help you KEEP GROWING!

THE
DYNAMIC CATHOLIC
INSTITUTE

[MISSION]

At Dynamic Catholic, it is our mission to re-energize
the Catholic Church in America by developing world-class
resources that inspire people to rediscover
the genius of Catholicism.

[VISION]

Our vision is to become the innovative leader in the
New Evangelization, helping Catholics and their parishes
become the-best-version-of-themselves.

We are passionate about re-energizing the Catholic Church in
America. To accomplish our mission, we believe we have to present
the faith in ways that are engaging and inspiring.

If the Church is to become vibrant again, it is of vital importance
we begin thinking on a whole new level.

At Dynamic Catholic, our story is just beginning.
We hope you choose to join us in it.